John K Genda

God's Blessings for Single Mothers

John K Genda

© 2021

All Scripture is taken from the King James Version (KJV), Public Domain

Editing by Savannah Cottrell - The Wonder Edits (www.thewonderedits.com)

Copyright © 2021 John K Genda Publishing

All rights reserved. No part of this book may be reproduced in any form or by any electronic or mechanical means, including information storage and retrieval systems, without permission in writing from the publisher.

Published by JKG Publishing

ISBN: 978-0-9747224-6-7

Visit http://www.johngenda.org/

Dear Beloved Single Mothers in the Lord,

Greetings to you from God our Father Who has reconciled us to Himself through our Lord and Savior, Jesus Christ.

I write to encourage my sisters in Christ who are in the state of single motherhood. Although this circumstance is common, the challenge of single motherhood is unique to each mother. Despite the challenges, I want to let single mothers know that the power of grace is available to look past the conditions, overcome the obstacles, and experience the blessings of God in Christ Jesus.

This book encourages single mothers to see and experience sufficiency in the power of grace to take them to a place of peace, stability, and wholeness and to receive the grace that has been made available to them by God our Father through the Lord Jesus Christ. Regardless of their condition or situation, they can be encouraged by the Word of God that there is a power more potent to overcome their condition, situation, hurt, pain, or challenge.

I want to let single mothers know that hurts can be healed, strife can turn to peace, and challenges can be overcome by His divine power. The power of Christ enables single mothers to lead a victorious life.

In Christ Jesus, the blessings of Abraham are made available to all by faith. Single mothers, place your faith in Jesus, and let your children receive the blessings of Abraham. Because of Abraham, God blessed Hagar, a single mother, and her son (Genesis 16). Because of Jesus Christ, God will bless you and your children.

Finally, single mothers who have repented, turned to Christ, and are blessed by Him should remember to strengthen other single mothers who do not know Christ by bringing them to be blessed, too. Share the blessings of Christ. Let single mothers know that because of Jesus, they and their children can be blessed.

May God richly bless you and your children.

With the love of Christ,

JOHN K GENDA

DEDICATION

To the only wise God, our Savior, be glory, majesty, dominion, and power, both now and forever. Amen.

John K Genda

FROM THE AUTHOR

This book is not the Bible. I have done my best with the help of the Spirit to bring clarity to some passages with the sincere purpose of drawing us closer to God. The goal is not to show my understanding of Scripture nor the Scriptures' authority. I am not an authority. The goal is to point professing Christians to the path of the cross and to lead the sinner to grace and repentance.

Although I am afraid to make a mistake, I am still humanly liable to errors. I encourage you to use your Bible and check Scriptures to ensure that you don't fall into human errors and that Scriptures are applied for what God wants, rather than what we want.

Let us learn the habits of the Berean Christians in Acts 17:11, who searched scriptures to verify preaching or what they hear:

"These were more noble than those in Thessalonica, in that they received the word with all readiness of mind, and searched the scriptures daily, whether those things were so."

As stated in Scripture since the beginning, what God wants should be the foundation of interpretation. Searching for Scriptures and altering them to fit our perversions were never God's intention for Biblical studies. God is Holy in both the New and Old Testaments. If we approach Scripture focusing on what God wants and not based on our natural desires and human natures, our errors will be minimal.

It is my prayer that we would be humble enough to approach scripture by seeking what God wants rather than seeking what you want to get out of Scripture to appease yourself.

May God richly bless you and your family.

John K Genda

Table of Contents

Dear beloved single mothers in the Lord 3

Dedication 5

From the Author 6

Moving Past the Circumstance 11

Dealing with the Challenge 20

The Blessings in Christ 31

When a Dead Situation Meets Resurrection Power 42

Seeking Life at the State of the Cross 51

Useful Practices that Lead to Divine Favor 55

    First 56
    Family 57
    Forsake 58
    Forward 59
    Forgive 60
    Forget 61
    Focus 62
    Freedom 62
    Find 63
    Faith 63

Fasting	*64*
Fellowship	*64*
Furnish	*66*
Fight	*66*
Finally	*67*
About the Author	*69*

John K Genda

GOD'S BLESSINGS FOR SINGLE MOTHERS

MOVING PAST THE CIRCUMSTANCE

Now Sarai Abraham's wife bare him no children: and she had an handmaid, and Egyptian, whose name was Hagar.

And Sarai said unto Abram, Behold now, the Lord hath restrained me from bearing: I pray thee, go in unto my maid; it may be that I may obtain children by her. And Abram hearkened to the voice of Sarai.

And Sarai Abram's wife took Hagar her maid the Egyptian, after Abram had dwelt ten years in the land of Canaan, and gave her to her husband Abram to be his wife.

And he went in unto Hagar, and she conceived: and when she saw that she had conceived, her mistress was despised in her eyes.

And Sarai said unto Abram, My wrong be upon thee: I have given my maid into thy bosom; and when she saw that she had conceived, I was despised in her eyes: the Lord judge between me and thee.

But Abram said unto Sarai, Behold, thy maid is in thy hand; do to her as it pleaseth thee. And when Sarai dealt hardly with her, she fled from her face.

> And the angel of the Lord found her by a fountain of water in the wilderness, by the fountain in the way to Shur.
>
> And he said, Hagar, Sarai's maid, whence camest thou? And whither wilt thou go? And she said, I flee from the face of my mistress Sarai.
>
> And the angel of the Lord said unto her, Return to thy mistress, and submit thyself under her hands.
>
> And the angel of the Lord said unto her, I will multiply thy seed exceedingly, that it shall not be numbered for multitude.
>
> And the angel of the Lord said unto her, Behold, thou art with child and shalt bear a son, and shalt call his name Ishmael; because the Lord hath heard thy affliction.
>
> **Genesis 16:1-11**

There are different circumstances through which a woman can become a single mother, such as disappointment, unfaithfulness, spousal abuse, death of a spouse, confusion, or having children outside of a marriage. We can't focus on judging the condition of singleness based on the event that caused the situation. The event is past, and we must look forward to the life ahead. The past is gone, and it will never return. There is nothing we can do to bring past human behaviors to our present lives. There is nothing we can do in our own power in reversing our past circumstances.

Some people are shocked when unexpected circumstances actually happen to them. The practical reality of single motherhood is not the same for all, and it can be more difficult for some than others.

As people try to figure out what's going on in their lives, they experience intense problems, instability, and pain. When people who are already in a messy or difficult situation come to God, we do not need to know everything about their situation or circumstance. Our purpose is to help direct them to the healing power of God.

Jesus came to heal the brokenhearted; that includes any single mother whose heart may have been broken or is still broken. "He hath sent me to heal the brokenhearted" (Luke 4:18). The event has already occurred, so the focus is not the circumstance. The focus is healing and blessings from a loving and available God Who sees and understands the pain of all. If the same power that raised Jesus from the dead lives in us, we would be in much better position to help direct people to Jesus, Who is able to restore and bless any life in any shape, circumstance or condition. There is no problem too great for God. "Is any thing too hard for the Lord? At the time appointed I will return unto thee, according to the time of life, and Sarah shall have a son" (Genesis 18:14).

There is nothing we can do in reversing a past circumstance in our own power. Satan wants us to focus on the circumstance that got us to the problem and to forget that God is able to bring us out of any circumstance. There is no life too messy, confused, broken, or sad for God to clean and bless. God is specialized in solving problems we can't solve and giving us rest in painful situations. We do not need to focus on the state in which people happen to be trapped. God is able to bring them to Himself and bring them to His love, His grace, His mercy, and His purpose. So, when we talk about the circumstance, we do not need to focus on the actions of people that created it. We need to instead focus on what God is able to do to bring them out of their tribulations.

The focus of God's grace is not how wicked or how sinful people are or have been. It is not about how bad the mistakes people have made or how bad people have acted. God's grace centers upon the desperate desire to receive and live the holy life of grace.

I say again, regardless of the circumstances, God is able to heal the brokenhearted. Satan wants to bind and keep single mothers in their conditions. Satan has no good intention for single mothers and their children. God wants to relieve the burdens that created their strife and take them instead to a blessed place through His Son Jesus Christ. Satan wants single mothers to stay focused on themselves to forget what God can do for them. God wants single mothers to come to Him. He wants to give them beauty for ashes: "To appoint unto them that mourn in Zion, to give unto them beauty for ashes" (Isaiah 61:3a).

God's Blessings for Single Mothers

Can you come? Can you give up yourself for the cross?

Biblical examples of single mothers include Hagar and one of the wives of the prophets whose husband served Elisha.

There are so many real-life examples of circumstances that caused women to become single mothers. The most common circumstance today, in my opinion, that leads to single motherhood is that of the unwed mother. Every day, around the world, more and more women are having children outside of marriage. The age group for these women begins very early.

I am very familiar with single unwed motherhood, because I had the opportunity to serve as an advocate for such women. I have had a lot of conversations with these women in regards to their circumstances. In one particular conversation with a young lady, I learned that she was very upset with her baby's father. She informed me that earlier in her pregnancy, everything was okay between her and her baby's father, but as time went along, and she was about six months pregnant, the baby's father began to distance himself from her. He got involved with other girls. Because of her experience, this young lady became very angry with men.

Another real-life example was that of a faithful Christian mother whose faith and stability was tested as she suddenly realized her state as a single mother. This woman was very blessed and happy with her marriage. Those of us who knew and saw the couple together admired them very much. They looked good together as a couple. They served in the church together. They did everything together. Everything appeared to be just okay. They were both leaders in the church. One day, the unexpected happened: the husband walked away. They were not newlyweds; they were married for several years. The wife was very shocked and disappointed. The most painful thing about the situation was that they were both leaders in the church, and they heard the Word of God regularly. I had no idea of the details or which party was responsible, but the point here is that a circumstance occurred, and the end result was single motherhood. Can you imagine the pain and shame this lady experienced as she stayed within the church after the husband left?

Most of us who have been in the church for a while know how "self-righteous" Christians think and respond to others in difficult circumstances. They sometimes have no feelings for the pain of others. Instead of the focus being directed to loving and restoring those in need, they will become talebearers. They will speculate the circumstance and subtly make it the topic of discussion for Bible studies and the sermon on Sunday morning. It is one issue when people see or notice problems before separation and another issue when everything appears to be good. The incident of a mate just walking away unexpectedly, regardless of the issues, indicates a serious and painful situation underneath that none of us would ever know and should not wish to know, either. Such disappointment, pain, and confusion can result in shock and denial that can knock a mother off her feet and turn her whole world upside down. Although we may not know who or what contributed to the situation, it is usually caused by a circumstance involving people. Our role as Christians is to focus on keeping people in the church by demonstrating the excessive love of Christ. The extreme love of Christ goes beyond what humanity expects of others. Without Christ, none of us can do anything.

Let us take an in-depth look at some Biblical circumstances that led mothers to single motherhood.

The sixteenth and twenty-first chapters of Genesis speak about Hagar. The circumstance of Hagar began with the impatience and attitude of Sarah. It was Sarah who gave Hagar to Abraham as a wife (she encouraged her husband to commit adultery, because she needed a child). Hagar did not marry Abraham by choice; Sarah gave her to Abraham. It was very common for a wife to give her maid to her husband in those days. The same Sarah who gave Hagar to Abraham as a wife was not mature enough to be patient with her. Back then, ungodly tradition (polygamy was not approved by God) allowed for the main wife, or the husband's favorite, to choose another wife for her husband for reasons best known to them. Sarah became jealous of Hagar, because she was pregnant and was going to have a baby for Abraham. As a result, she began to mistreat Hagar. She desired to get rid of Hagar, and she waited for an opportunity to present itself. The opportunity finally came through Ishmael. This time, Sarah was determined to kick Hagar out. Hagar's attitude towards her mistress was not good, either.

These are some of the things that happen when we try to help bring God's promise to reality with unrighteous human effort that is so clear.

Hagar had no choice but to leave. Hagar became a single mother as a result of attitudes, contentions, and the sins of human nature. This included the attitudes of Hagar, Abraham, Sarah, and Ishmael. The whole situation was sin, and the end was sin. Even though what transpired between Abraham, Sarah, and Hagar was not God's will, God still had mercy and compassion. This is because "while we were yet sinners, Christ died for us" (Romans 5:8b). Hagar's circumstance and situation were messy, but God has mercy (Genesis 16:11). The focus is not the circumstance, but, instead, it is the resurrection power of God, which is able to touch any circumstance.

God saw Hagar's situation when she was still in trouble and pain. The intensity of your situation or struggle is unable to block God's view and will. God wants to help you. Whether the situation is hopeless, or whether you are bound by any form of addiction, God is able to free you. God saw the messy situation. He heard the cry of Hagar and responded by offering help. Oh, I wish we could have the attitude of God to respond to the crying, pain, and distress of others.

Another Biblical circumstance that led a woman to single motherhood is in the fourth chapter of Second Kings. This woman was the wife of a prophet. She had a good relationship with her husband, but unfortunately, her husband died. She had no choice but to face the challenges of being a single mother. She was left in heavy debt and two sons. She had no way out, and no one could help her, but God showed up again, just as He did for Hagar. I pray that God would show up in your time of need.

We can list circumstance after circumstance that led to the situation of single motherhood, but our focus is never the situation. Instead, we should look to a God Who is able to turn our failures into a life we never imagined. The focus should not be the circumstance or who is right or wrong. The focus should be on searching for a God Who sees every pain and heals the broken heart. The goal of single motherhood should be looking past the trials, embracing the challenge through the cross, and expecting the blessed life that flows from the cross.

The focus here is reaching out to single mothers and showing them how can they best serve God and receive His blessings moving forward and how can we help them take the cross that Christ gives daily.

John K Genda

DEALING WITH THE CHALLENGE

And the child grew, and was weaned: and Abraham made a great feast the same day that Isaac was weaned.

And Sarah saw the son of Hagar the Egyptian, which she had born unto Abraham, mocking.

Wherefore she said unto Abraham, cast out this bondwoman and her son: for the son of this bondwoman shall not be heir with my son, even with Isaac.

And the thing was very grievous in Abraham's sight because of his son.

And God said unto Abraham, Let it not be grievous in thy sight because of the lad, and because of thy bondwoman; in all that Sarah hath said unto thee, hearken unto her voice; for in Isaac shall thy seed be called.

And also of the son of the bondwoman will I make a nation, because he is thy seed.

And Abraham rose up early in the morning, and took bread, and a bottle of water, and gave it unto Hagar, putting it on her shoulder, and the child, and sent her

> away: and she departed, and wandered in the wilderness of Beersheba.
>
> And the water was spent in the bottle, and she cast the child under one of the shrubs.
>
> And she went, and sat her down over against him a good way off, as it were a bow shot: for she said, Let me not see the death of the child. And she sat over against him, and lift up her voice, and wept.
>
> And God heard the voice of the lad; and the angel of God called to Hagar out of heaven, and said unto her, What aileth thee, Hagar? fear not; for God hath heard the voice of the lad where he is.
>
> Arise, lift up the lad, and hold him in thine hand; for I will make him a great nation.
>
> And God opened her eyes, and she saw well of water; and she went, and filled the bottle with water, and gave the lad drink.
>
> And God was with the lad; and he grew, and dwelt in the wilderness, and became an archer.
>
> And he dwelt in the wilderness of Paran: and his mother took him a wife out of the land of Egypt.
>
> **Genesis 21:8-21**

Most single mothers are often faced with the challenge of rearing children on limited resources. In most cases, the father, who is usually supposed to be a major resource, is never around, and the mother is left to seek other sources of help. This leaves the mother with limited time and an ongoing need for childcare and support.

The endeavors of single mothers to love, protect, provide, and nurture their children oftentimes lead to exhaustion, frustration, and other emotional problems. The demand that the job and hustle both put on single mothers, as well as the demands of the kids, also exacts a toll on their bodies. Both kids and parents also have to deal with emotional and affectional issues, especially in cases where custody is a problem. As shown in the previous chapter, the struggle of Hagar is a good Biblical example of the challenges of a single mother.

I used to work with a single mother who had two children. I saw the exhaustion on her face when she came to work. She would come to work late sometimes, because she had no choice due to the unexpected things that would come up with her kids. Those who have or have had small children may understand what I am talking about. This is an educated young lady who desires to get to work on time. The emergencies of her children sometimes just didn't permit her to be on time some days, including babysitters changing their minds, children getting sick, and teachers calling from the school for kids to be picked up. She received child support payments, but rearing children involves more than monetary child support. She was always on the run, which caused her to rush her work and become stressed on the job.

The challenge of teenage mothers is probably the hardest of all single mothers. Most times, their baby's father rejects them before the baby is born. As a result, sometimes, these young sisters begin to get headaches. They feel so alone. They get angry, upset, and afraid. The pain of rejection, confusion, and suffering affects young mothers, because the expecting fathers are nowhere to be found.

The issue of an absent father is of great significance. But thank God for being a Father to the fatherless (Psalm 68:5a). As some children grow up, they will begin to seek the need for their fathers. Mothers deal with this particular emotional and affectional issue at different times in the lives of their children. Some mothers just avoid the question, especially when they are still mad and angry. The work of God in forgiveness is needed in this area. The Spirit of the living God will give direction in this situation that will give peace to all parties involved. Getting out of self and what we want and allowing God to lead is the only solution. We will cause more problems like Sarah if we go by human sense rather than God's principles.

Childcare and healthcare issues also need to be considered. These are issues that almost every parent faces. The lack of the right babysitter or funds needed to provide a babysitter often results in further problems. Leaving children alone can also lead to long-term destructive consequences. Some situations can be more difficult and complex to handle than others. I have seen a situation in which a teenage sibling was forced to assume the responsibility of a parent by always babysitting and missing school. This youngster was babysitting when he was supposed to be in class. I found out by making a home visit to this teenage boy's residence, because he was always late for school and missing many days from classes.

Some professional single mothers are blessed to have jobs with good benefits. Their careers help to cover the mostly unaffordable cost of health and child care. In contrast, single mothers in need are forced to depend on the state for the healthcare needs of their children.

Custody issues where children are involved are a common challenge in the modern world. They are very sensitive and painful situations as children are torn apart. Some parents have managed to work things out in a manner that focuses on the best interest of the children. Even with the best situations, there are still challenges, because it was never God's intention from the beginning for parents to be separated.

The situation is different for everyone. But how can this challenge be handled so that forward progress can be made and be the focus? What can you do on your part to make a broken family situation work best? This type of challenge can only be resolved in a manner that leads to peace by believing and depending on the work of God through the Holy Spirit. God is able to restore a broken and shattered life, and He is able to minimize the impact of the damage on children and mothers as well. This is a challenge that requires the people involved to take their life out of the issue and give it to God. God knows the best situation for the kids, and His ways must be followed.

One of the most important resources in which single mothers are usually limited is time. Whether we believe it or not, time is one of the most important resources that one can have. Time is money. Time is more important than child support. It is more important than money and social service. A single mother may have all the other things she needs, but if she has no time for her children, she will not be at rest.

I once had a dialogue with a single mother of two children. She wanted to pursue higher educational or professional training.

The first question I asked her was, "Who is going to watch your children?"

She replied, "They are at an age where they can take care of themselves."

The children were barely teenagers at the time. I know her first priority was not to leave the children unsupervised, but that was her last choice and only option.

None of us need to be a rocket scientist to know that children are affected negatively without proper adult supervision at all times. These days, it is a common thing for children as young as eight years old to be left alone after school until their mom gets home from work. The outcome can be very challenging to both parents and kids.

For some single mothers, dealing with a child's father can be very challenging in certain situations. This creates the baby father drama. Those involved in the baby father or baby mother drama usually make it so, because they forget about the ultimate goal for and the best interest of the child. This can be quite a challenge for most single mothers to handle, depending on their circumstance. But if things are handled based on what God wants, a solution can be attained that works for all involved.

The challenge of Hagar as a single mother began when she was driven to the wilderness. Anyone who has the compassion of God will be touched by the struggles of Hagar. She was driven out of Abraham's household with nothing but a bottle of water and a loaf of bread to live on for the rest of her life (Genesis 21:14). Also, imagine the emotional challenges, such as the tension of Sarah, the distress of Abraham as his affection for his son is shattered, and the perseverance of Hagar as a single mother with nothing. She wandered in the wilderness with her son. The word "wilderness" brings to mind a place of trial and demonic activity. Hagar was in a place where there was nothing: no people, no friends, and not even a television to watch or radio to listen to. There was no social media at the time to share her story or to connect to people. Grandma was not present to help, and social services were not available at the time. All she had around her were trees and wild animals. Abraham never made arrangements for the child for her. Hagar was in a place of pain, suffering, distress, starvation, and agony.

It is human nature to mourn our struggles, especially when they become incredibly intense. Hagar understood that focusing on her struggles was not the answer, though. She began to cry to God for her blessings. She cried for her son, until God heard her son crying (Genesis 21:17). When her resources ran out, God stepped in to make a way in an environment where she could not see her way out.

Ignoring the issue of single motherhood within churches is another huge challenge. Not every single mother has been delivered from pain and hurt. Responding to the trials of single mothers can be a challenge in itself for church leadership or ministries if not done tactfully with the help of the Holy Spirit. Some churches just ignore single mothers altogether and act as if they do not exist. The role of churches or ministries can be very important in helping single mothers stay in the path of the cross. A church or ministry may not meet every challenge they face, but they can help alleviate some of the burdens. It is not the duty of the church to make conclusions based on circumstances a single mother may be found in, but, instead, they should help bring them to a better place in God. Churches need to make informed decisions in these matters. Discernment is needed when dealing with single mothers on a case-by-case basis. It takes a lot of determination and sacrifice for single mothers to follow the lead of the Holy Spirit and live for God, hence the need for ministry to them in a loving and caring manner.

Single mothers already have challenges, but coming together as a church can alleviate the struggles they face. Some people don't ask for help, so we need to stop asking people if they need help to let us know when we know they need help. It is easy to sense when people need aid if we are walking in the ways of God.

What are we doing as a church to address the state of single motherhood? As the body of Christ (1 Corinthians 12:27), we can't keep asking people all the time whether they need help; we should see the need and help according to our ability. We need to learn to give what we have according to the need and our ability.

Nowadays, the challenge of single mothers is much more complex, and people are not willing or attempting to help them in most cases. They wickedly say, *Who told you to have kids?* in their hearts. They miss the side of Christ that cries, *That's Me! Have mercy on Me!* (Matthew 25:34-40). Even though churches may have the resources to help some mothers, they will just say, "I am praying for you."

Let us think of how life can be difficult for two parents and how much more for a single mother.

God appreciates when we give from the bottom of our hearts and not when people are looking at us (Luke 18:9-14). It is more appreciative of God when we attend to a need without being asked. Giving is not just handing over money or things. People need to be given affection and time. This is a task the women of the church should take on. A loving and caring atmosphere can be a great tool in addressing the needs of single mothers and making them part of God's family.

Single mothers have several challenges that may affect their relationship and fellowship with God. Less fortunate single mothers may need a ride to church, and some may need clothing for their kids, as well as money for school activities, bus trips, school supplies, warm food and clothing, gym outfits for school, transportation for extracurricular activities, tutoring, and lots of little things that we may not even be aware of.

The church has two roles in addressing the needs of single mothers: the role of dealing with physical needs and the role of dealing with spiritual needs. Both of these needs should always be addressed. Jesus usually addressed the physical needs of the people who came to Him, while He also addressed their spiritual needs. The Gospel addresses both physical and spiritual needs, too.

How the church addresses such needs is the issue; most churches do not have all the resources to address every physical need, but they can do little things to make a difference, as long as the issue of single motherhood is not ignored within the church.

There are some good churches that do not have a ministry for single motherhood. Nevertheless, women as a whole within the church can do something to address the issue. If you are in a good church that does not address the issues of single motherhood, then that can be a ministry for you; this would be not only a ministry to seek help, but also a ministry to reach out to single mothers who may not be in the church.

The spiritual needs of single mothers are of the utmost importance, because if they are not spiritually sound, they will be unable to help their children and themselves. There would be no stability in their lives. The two single mothers from the Old Testament whom we have spoken of in this book have had some form of spiritual connection in the height of their agony and distress. If they knew how to cry unto God, we also can cry unto Him today in times of need and distress.

The goal of the church is to help people cry to God to establish a connection with Him, not with the pastor or his wife. People need to know that God is the greatest help they can get. We should understand that God can use any means to bless us.

THE BLESSINGS IN CHRIST

Now the Lord had said unto Abram, Get thee out of thy country, and from thy kindred, and from thy father's house, unto a land that I will shew thee:

And I will make of thee a great nation, and I will bless thee, and make thy name great; and thou shalt be a blessing:

And I will bless them that bless thee, and curse him that curseth thee: and in thee shall all families of the earth be blessed.

Genesis 12:1-3

There is neither Jew nor Greek, there is neither bond nor free, there is neither male nor female: for ye are all one in Christ Jesus.

And if ye be Christ's, then are ye Abraham's seed, and heirs according to the promise.

Galatians 3:28-29

Now there cried a certain woman of the wives of the sons of the prophets unto Elisha, saying, Thy servant my husband is dead; and thou knowest that thy servant did fear the Lord: and the creditor is come to take unto him my two sons to be bondmen.

And Elisha said unto her, What shall I do for thee? tell me, what hast thou in the house? And she said, Thine handmaid hath not any thing in the house, save a pot of oil.

Then he said, Go, borrow thee vessels abroad of all thy neighbours, even empty vessels; borrow not a few.

And when thou art come in, thou shalt shut the door upon thee and upon thy sons, and shalt pour out into all those vessels, and thou shalt set aside that which is full.

So she went from him, and shut the door upon her and upon her sons, who brought the vessels to her; and she poured out.

And it came to pass, when the vessels were full, that she said unto her son, Bring me yet a vessel. And he said unto her, There is not a vessel more. And the oil stayed.

Then she came and told the man of God. And he said, Go, sell the oil, and pay thy debt, and live thou and thy children of the rest.

2 Kings 4:1-7

God's Blessings for Single Mothers

All single mothers who are in Christ Jesus have access to the same blessings that God gave Abraham. These blessings can include, but are not limited to, righteousness, divine favor, expansion, sustenance, godly popularity (known because of the works of God), a husband, a career, a business, peace, joy, the prosperity of godly children, and much more.

Hagar was blessed, because she was connected to Abraham and his covenant-keeping God. The Bible makes it clear that anyone connected to Jesus Christ through faith is a child of Abraham and has access to the blessings God originally gave him.

In order for a single mother to access the blessings of Abraham, she must be connected to Jesus Christ. He is the link to the blessings of Abraham. For example, in order to move from one page to another in a web site, we must activate or touch a hyperlink. As we touch that link of the place or address we want to go to, it takes us right there. A link does not work by itself. It can only take us to the next location if activated by touch. Jesus can only take us to experience the blessings of God if we accept Him. We must give all our affection, passions, and emotions to Jesus. We must love Him with all our hearts, souls, and minds. We must go through Jesus Christ and by no other way.

Single mothers who desire to move on to a new page in their lives must be connected to Christ. After they do so, then they will ask, and they shall receive; they will knock, and the door will be open; they will seek, and they will find (Matthew 7:7)! Because of the finished work of the cross and the resurrection of Christ, we now have a better covenant than Abraham did.

Two major blessings of Abraham for single mothers in Christ are righteousness and prosperity. Although the message of prosperity has been abused by so many as greed, the Bible, from Genesis to Revelation, promises those who love God good things. The blessings of Abraham come in various forms. They are not just limited to material prosperity. These blessings involve the prosperity of the soul body and spirit. We must give up ourselves, take up the cross of Jesus Christ, and follow Him to truly understand the blessings of God that no one else can give (Matthew 16:24).

Despite the challenges of the cross and the blessings we may not readily experience, taking the cross itself brings internal peace that prospers the soul. When the soul prospers, everything else will follow. When single mothers believe and have faith in God, their children will walk in righteousness and prosperity of the cross. Their children will not sell and use drugs, and the girls will not prostitute themselves.

Prosperity and righteousness are related. It was only after Abraham believed the word of God that God declared him to be righteous. God is waiting to declare every single mother who believes in Jesus Christ as righteous.

Righteousness leads to the prosperity of God. Prosperity, in this case, means having enough for your family and for others. God wants us to have more than just enough. People will only know that God is blessing us when we are able to share prosperity with them. It was this same blessing of Abraham that Hagar and her son experienced. Hagar moved from a bare bottle of water and a loaf of bread to a lifetime provision of water. The divine well never runs out.

Blessings are available to every single mother who is connected to Christ. Now, because of the blood of Jesus, single mothers have a much better covenant!

Here are some more blessings of Abraham that we can consider:

- *The blessing of growth and expansion.* God will cause you and your children to grow and expand when you stay connected to Him. Your children will be intelligent and creative. They will excel in whatever they put their hands to do. Out of your children will come entrepreneurs, engineers, governors, preachers, pastors, evangelists, prophets, and so on. Their talents and abilities will multiply. Your children will own and control their own estates.
- *The blessing of popularity.* This is no way to hide when you begin to multiply in talents and creativity or substance. You

don't need to announce yourself. You will be popular, not because of your ability, but because of God Almighty through His Son Jesus. People will seek your autograph, because they will hear about you. Your name will be in the news for good things. God will make your name great! God blessed Abraham, Isaac, and Jacob, and He expanded them. He did the same thing for Ishmael due to his connection to Abraham. He will do the same for your children if you accept the ways of God through Jesus Christ and teach your children to do likewise.

- ***The blessing of divine favor.*** God will give you and your children favor. He will open doors for your children. He will give them what money can't buy. He will connect them to the people who can give them what they want. The Holy Scriptures tell us that God will fulfill every good desire for His glory. God blesses us not for ourselves but to display His glory.

The blessings of Abraham in the Old Testament were a signal for greater blessings Christ will give those who accept Him. Hagar did not seem to have an affection for God as Abraham did, but Hagar was connected to Abraham, who knew God was Who mattered. The connection to Christ through Whom God the Father blesses the world is Who matters.

God's Blessings for Single Mothers

In her struggles as a single mother, Hagar cried to God for help. Hagar had a need. She had no time for foolishness and gossip. She was desperate for help, and she called out to God. She made a connection to God. All single mothers who desire the blessings of God must know how to cry to God. God heard her cry and opened her eyes to begin to see and experience His blessings.

If you are in Christ, the "blessings of Abraham" are already around you. You can't experience it if your spiritual eyes are still closed. Your eyes need to be open for you to see your blessing. Only the Holy Spirit can cause one's natural eyes to be open. It is okay to cry for your eyes to be open.

Both Hagar and her son were about to die. They ran out of water in the wilderness. Though the water of God was around, Hagar could not drink it until God opened her eyes. God moved Hagar from temporary sustenance to lifetime provision. Hagar was at a place where she thought no one could help her. Her hope and expectation were outside the human realm. When all hope in humanity was lost, God showed up in time. God was always there.

You may be having a wilderness experience, a place of testing, trial, and demonic activity, like Hagar's. It seems as if your needs are just not being met. You are always broke and going through difficulties. Most single mothers find themselves in similar situations today, where the refrigerator might be empty, the gas tank is low, the mortgage or rent payments are due, or kids are outgrowing clothes and shoes. Sometimes, you may have no choice but to cry.

Your answer is right there. God has seen your tears. He will turn those tears into rivers of blessings. God is getting ready to open your eyes so that you can see your blessings. You will see what you have never seen in your lifetime. God wants you to be still and know that He is God (Psalm 46:10a).

God knew he was going to bless Hagar, because He had reaffirmed His promise to Abraham concerning Ishmael. God had promised that He was going to multiply Ishmael. But guess what? Ishmael's mother had to cry to get God's attention for the release. God knows our needs even before we ask, just as God knew Hagar's needs before she called to Him.

All this was because Ishmael was the seed of Abraham and entitled to his blessings, just as we are entitled to those same blessings, because we are in Christ.

Let me remind you again: if you are in Christ, you are entitled to the unlimited blessings of Abraham. Learn to be a child of Abraham in Christ by faith to the point that Jesus will say: "Daughter, thy faith hath made thee whole" (Mark 5:34a). Single mothers, I encourage you to cry to God, and He will bless you. Get in Christ Jesus and live by faith. He came to give you hope. Be confident that God is faithful to His promises. Sometimes, it may not come when you want it or how you want it, but as long as you are connected to Christ, it will come in ways you do not expect. Blessings go way beyond materialism.

"God is not a man, that he should lie" (Numbers 23:19a). Although the situation was messy, God didn't fail Abraham when it came to blessing his children. God blessed both the child of promise and the child of the bondwoman, because He made a covenant with Abraham. Regardless of your messy past or condition, as long as you are in Christ and following His commandments, God accepts you. This is why the church should not classify people based on their circumstances. The church should understand that the blessings of Abraham are available to all those who accept Christ.

As a mother, Hagar did not want to watch her baby die. God came not only to respond to Hagar, but also her child. Even though Ishmael was not a promise child, God went ahead and promised blessing on the vulnerable baby boy. God cares for the defenseless and downtrodden. Even though people contribute to their own problems, God still cares. God's mercy is so powerful to the point that no human can understand.

Let us turn our attention back to the widow woman in the fourth chapter of Second Kings. This widow was experiencing difficult times in her life. She was in debt. She had no options or resources at all. She needed divine intervention. The creditor came to take her two sons as collateral to satisfy debts by enslaving them. This woman had no means of repaying her creditor. Today, we would say that this woman was bankrupt. The only asset this woman had was a pot of oil. She didn't realize that the oil was symbolic of Christ, the Anointed One. Spiritually, this woman was connected to Christ, being a seed of Abraham. I want you to understand that Christ has been around since the beginning with the Father (John 1:1). Though this woman had the anointing all along, she never used it.

Thank God for Elisha the prophet, who instructed the widow how to use the anointing to solve her problems. Imagine that you are going to a man of God for help, and that man asks you about what you have in your house. You might think that the man of God is crazy, especially when you are in a desperate situation. However, the widow understood Elisha's request by her faith, and God blessed her obedience. As this woman began to use the only oil she had, it multiplied. This widow was so blessed that she had enough oil to sell and pay off her debt, and she was able to live off the rest of the money.

What do you have in your house as a single mother? What do you have that God can multiply to meet all your needs? What talents do you have that you do not know? What abilities do you have that you have not used? What are the spiritual connections that God has placed in your life to lead you to your promised land?

Let us remember to go past the circumstances and challenges and start expecting the best from God. You will be surprised to discover what God has placed within you that can change your life, but you must surrender your life and ways of self to Christ Jesus. Cry to Him, and He will open your eyes to see what's around you and what's within you that He can use to multiply and bring you an increase!

John K Genda

WHEN A DEAD SITUATION MEETS RESURRECTION POWER

I want to encourage single mothers never to give up if they happen to find themselves in a dead situation, one in which they have absolutely no power to control or change. The only solution is to keep hope alive. It is better to die hoping than to live without hope at all.

A dead situation is one in which human efforts and actions will not change the outcome. The only solution to a dead situation is resurrection power, which is credited to only God the Father through Christ. Even a dead situation has its Master. When resurrection power meets a dead situation, the latter comes to life. The same resurrection power that raised Jesus from the dead is available to deal with any dead situation.

The resurrection power is a miracle-working power. It was this same power that breathed life into dirt, and out of that dirt came Adam. The resurrection power has always been the same yesterday, today, and forever. Miracles could only be done by resurrection power (Romans 8:11). Regardless of how dead the situation may be, it is only dead until it meets resurrection power. When it touches a dead situation, it will come to life. The essence of the cross is the power of the resurrection. It is important for us to understand the significance of the cross and the resurrection. As Ezekiel prophesied to the dry bones, they came to life as a result of power flowing to death (Ezekiel 37:1-14).

There are several forms of dead situations we may face in this life. Some are in dead situations with their careers. Exploring and exhausting all human efforts, paying our bills, raising healthy kids, obtaining employment, sickness, and more can be dead situations, and the list will go on and on. We may find ourselves in a time where to even pay the bills may be dead, and there is no way out.

Most of us have been in situations where everything seems to be dead or not working at all. Things may not only seem dead, but they also may seem hopeless. As human beings, we are always going to be faced with these kinds of situations in various forms. We have seen people with tons of money who faced a dead situation with sickness that only resurrection power can heal. Their wealth was unable to heal them or bring them back to life. There is nothing our own brains and abilities can do about certain problems. The solution to uncertainty is supernatural. There is absolutely nothing we can do about a dead situation but to mourn it. Dead situations make us cry and feel pain and loss. Some problems are beyond our brains and capabilities. Our power can only operate within our limited ability!

The prophet's wife in Second Kings chapter four, a single mother, found herself in a dead situation that was beyond her control. Her husband, who was the provider for the home, was dead. Back in those days, most women were housewives. She had nothing to pay back her debt. She was in a dead situation over which self-help had no power. She happened to find itself in a situation that she could not resolve on her own. The widow faced a very difficult state as the creditors came to take her two sons as collateral for her debts. Thank God for divine intervention that they were not taken. In a similar way, we may find ourselves in situations where everything may seem dead to us, but they are only dead until they meet resurrection power.

As we know, when resurrection power touches any dead situation, it comes to life. The situation of the wife of one of the prophets was only dead until she met resurrection power. Hagar's messy circumstance was only dead until resurrection power stepped in. Your situation may only be dead until it comes in contact with resurrection power. The end of your torment will stop at resurrection power.

Resurrection power is the proof of the unlimited power of God and the proof of the divinity of Jesus Christ. Human power stops at death, but resurrection power begins at death. At the death of any situation, the possibility of human power ceases to exist.

Most times, we feel hopeless upon experiencing a dead situation. At that point, we are powerless, and all we know is to mourn. We mourn because we are at the place of death where human power is useless. We mourn the fact that our human and intellectual ability is dead. Such abilities lack resurrection power. All we do is mourn at a dead situation, because we see no other available option outside resurrection power. Upon realizing that a situation is dead, the only action we have strength to take is to mourn it by crying for divine help or just grieving in pain and agony. Those who have been in a dead situation know what I am talking about. The mourning can involve tears and complete quietness. And sometimes, we are tempted to isolate ourselves, as there seems to be no help. But even in the midst of tears, divine reassurance is there.

Regardless of how strong our will or resolve is, we sometimes find ourselves in situations in which our willpower is unable to provide answers to our problems. We feel hopeless after we have done all we needed to do, but the situation remains the same. Assuming that we have done everything in our might and power and nothing changes, that's an indication that our only hope is resurrection power. Despite expending and exhausting our intellectual abilities, the situation still seems to be dead due to human limitation. One can be considered righteous and still face a dead-end situation.

Daniel in the lions' den is a classic example of this kind of situation when it comes to human ability (Daniel 6). It was a dead-end situation for Daniel as he was human, but it was not so for resurrection power. Resurrection power will shut the mouth of your lions or destroyers. There was nothing Daniel could do outside of prayer and fasting. If God did not intervene, the lions could have made Daniel a breakfast or dinner. It is only resurrection power that can shut the mouth of lions. This means that even God-fearing people do face dead-end situations.

The focus is to see the power of God resurrecting a dead situation and not on the circumstance that causes the situation. When we come to Christ, He looks past our messy conditions.

When the widow woman came to the prophet Elisha, he essentially asked her two questions: "What do you want me to do for you?" and "What do you have in your house?" This seems very similar to how Jesus dealt with people. Jesus always asked questions. The object for such questions was usually to see whether one has within them the faith to activate resurrection power. The widow did not realize she had the anointing of God within her house to activate that resurrection power. Her late husband was a prophet who feared God, so she had built her faith on Him. This is the same as Jesus saying "thy faith hath made thee whole" (Mark 5:34). When God looks from Heaven and sees us crying in faith, resurrection power is activated to move our dead situations. He responds in the most surprising and unexpected way we can imagine (Isaiah 61).

God knows how to bring a dead situation to life, and He does it how He wants, when He wants it, and where He wants it. Sometimes, He may even provide us directions to bringing a dead situation to life or bring life out of it. The widow took a faith action by contacting a man of God who clearly had a connection with Him.

If the same power that raised Jesus from the dead lives in us, we should be able to see things as God sees them. It can be very difficult to move forward without understanding of the power that raised Christ from the dead.

Being faithful to God is like a bank account. God is able to sustain us and lead us to resources until we are able to get back on our feet. Taking faith actions such as contacting praying people and also crying to God and expecting Him to help is beneficial. Faith actions should be initiated in the event of a dead situation to establish a connection with God. Relationships with God are essential in this case. Establishing a relationship with God by the Word and the people of faith is incredibly advantageous.

When we come to God, we must empty ourselves completely so that we can experience the new life that God wants us to have. The oil of God can only be poured into empty vessels. We have got to empty ourselves of our past hurts, pain, and trouble to be in the position of the resurrection power. The flowing of the resurrection power of God through Elisha was evidence of what God does as we empty ourselves. Wherever the cross is executed to deny self, the power of resurrection flows.

When we were crucified with Christ, even our stubborn will was crucified as well. We were in Christ when he was crucified on Calvary. He took our obstinate will of sin to the cross. Each day, we are in a situation demanding the exercise of our will, but we have to believe God by faith that our natural, sin-prone will was crucified with Christ.

Your ability to pay your bills may be dead. Even if you have worked hard, held two jobs, and worked overtime, the numbers still can add up to resolve your problem. Some have tried living a sanctified life, but they have failed time after time and reached the dead end of "I can't do it anymore."

Abraham was messed up. Sarah was messed up. Hagar was messed up, and the entire household was a mess. But in all the messy situations, there was still the mercy of God. As Christians, we do not need to look at people based on their situations, but instead based on what the resurrection power of God can do. This power is able to save and deliver from any problem. God is faithful, and we should not put limits on the saving power of God.

Dealing and responding to a dead situation is no laughing matter. Facing a dead situation means recognizing that we are at the point of desperation. We realize we have no means of solving a problem or resolving a situation without God's help.

The widow in Second Kings chapter four was at that point of desperation. She needed help, and she needed it right away, or her sons would be gone. Hagar was at a point of despair, and she needed help right away, or her son would die. In turn, we are at a point of despondency when facing eviction with small kids. It is a point of desperation when a child is sick, and the parent has no health insurance.

The wife of the prophet saw the cross as her first and only option by going straight to Elisha, the man of God. She could have gone to her friend or neighbor. We should not be putting anything before God. Our mates' children's blessings from God are good, but they can't help us. Sometimes, we worry about our kids, but our children are not more important than God Who gave them to us. There are times when we worship the blessing more than God of blessings. Our blessings may become our idols if we are not careful. If we don't look for the cross, and if we do not expect it when it comes, we will not recognize and accept it.

We usually don't ask for what God wants us to do for Him; we always ask what we want from God. We come to God when our minds are made up already based on our expectation. We ignore the cross when we rush to fulfill our own need before our need of God. It is very easy for desperation to arise when it seems our needs are not being met, but I want to encourage you to keep hope alive, even in the most difficult situations. God is still God, and He will give you peace to experience life without stress.

SEEKING LIFE AT THE STATE OF THE CROSS

Life at the state of the cross is an undisturbed life that comes from strengthening the inner man as we take the cross daily.

The prophetess Anna is a classic Biblical example of life at the state of the cross (Luke 2:36-39). Anna's life was not put in friends, pleasure, fashion, entertainment, or things. Her life was placed in only God. For us to experience the peace of God, we must take life out of the things we have placed them in and put our lives in God. He wants us to have peace and have it undisturbed at all times. True joy can only be realized when we get to that point of undisturbed peace (John 14:27). What we should do in getting to the point of undisturbed peace is the key.

The best place for any single mother to be is at the state of the cross. It is the state of being and living in the will of God. Living in the will of God involves emptying ourselves and letting God occupy us.

The Bible has a distinct account of a single widow, who found undisturbed life in the presence of God. She was Anna, the prophetess:

> And there was one Anna, a prophetess, the daughter of Phanuel, of the tribe of Aser: she was of a great age, and had lived with an husband seven years from her virginity;
>
> And she was a widow of about fourscore and four years, which departed not from the temple, but served God with fastings and prayers night and day.
>
> And she coming in that instant gave thanks likewise unto the Lord, and spake of him to all them that looked for redemption in Jerusalem.
>
> And when they had performed all things according to the law of the Lord, they returned into Galilee, to their own city Nazareth
>
> **Luke 2:36-39**

Anna emptied herself of herself. Emptying oneself of oneself can be very challenging for most of us. However, it prepares us for a resurrected life that empowers us to live a life of satisfaction. This life of satisfaction is a life directed by Heaven. Let us pause for a minute and think of all the things we want in life: what we wish to buy, the places we wish to go, the things we wish to enjoy, and the pleasure we wish to seek.

What if God shows up and says, "Everything you wish for yourself is not what I want for you"? What would you do? Would you proceed to do what you want, regardless of what God wants for your life? The point here is that God will not force us to choose the best He wants for us. If He did, then He would not hold us accountable for our choices. He will keep prompting us of sin and judgment, but the choice is absolutely ours.

We are exposed to so many images that we are attracted to, but we must have the courage to lean towards what God wants. The media in particular makes available to us so many things we may desire. These wishes are advertised as things that will bring satisfaction and happiness to us. They are promoted as must-be things, must-have things, and must-do things for complete happiness. Advertising usually plays to our natural person, the person we were born to be. If the sinful person of Adam was meant to make us happy, then these advertisements would not be necessary in the first place, because we would have already been in the state of happiness. But this is not true. These advertisements want to fill us so that we can live by their dictates of the continuous desire for more.

Some single mothers have not learned how to deny themselves, not even for their own children. They just want what they want, regardless of the consequences. Sometimes, this desire to go out of God's will based on what they had known slows down the blessings of God. I don't think Abraham would have been blessed had he not responded to the call of God in obedience. He could have ignored God's voice and continued living among his heathen relatives. He chose the blessings over the curse.

A lesson that can be learned from the prophetess Anna is that she chose to be in the presence of God. Her focus was building her spirit to connect with God, and her entire life was devoted to God. She practiced her devotion with prayer and fasting. She was known by others to be connected to God. It was her devotion to God that brought her complete satisfaction and led her to see the salvation of God. Devotion to God can bring complete peace and will lead to open doors in many areas of our lives.

You do not have to live in a physical temple like Anna the prophetess in order to stay in the presence of God. Your body is a temple of the Holy Spirit (1 Corinthians 6:19). You can worship God daily anywhere and everywhere in spirit and in truth (John 4:24). Allow the life of God to fill you by emptying yourself of earthly things in which you have placed your life. Empty yourself of anything that is not of God. Ask God to help you stay away from people, things, and events that lead to sin and unrighteousness. The effect of divine life of a parent can touch the children as well.

You will be filled with peace by getting rid of the self-life every day, taking a cross daily, and following Jesus. When you get rid of life that is not from God, He will rescue you, save you, and cause you to see and experience His salvation.

USEFUL PRACTICES THAT LEAD TO DIVINE FAVOR

There are always going to be problems in life to which we may not have all the answers, but we can engage certain practices to fuel us to move towards favor with God and people, eventually leading to a solution or stability.

Stability and serenity can be achieved through the Spirit in the midst of a challenging situation. There is no status in life exempted from the issues that life presents. From time to time, people will face similar circumstances in this life, whether they are Christians or not. The difference between the challenges of a Christian and that of a non-Christian is that the response of a Christian to the difficulties faced is based on what God wants, and the results are usually incredibly fulfilling regardless of how small or significant the outcome.

When Christians respond to situations according to what God wants, He deals with issues from within, as opposed to only dealing with problems externally. Naturally, we may not only see our way out or resolve every problem. With always desiring godly principles and asking God to strengthen our will to comply, we will experience peace as we live as works in progress. Never focus on big marvels right away. Celebrate the daily small victories and wonders.

Let us look at specific practices that will help move us towards favor or better results. We may not have all the answers or formulas, but we can accept what God wants for us.

FIRST

It has been a common practice of the devil to attack the families of single Christian mothers who forget to put God first in their own lives and the lives of their children. Though the devil will always attack, if God is first in our homes, the devil will not succeed.

For many years, people have been deceived to believe that putting God first is just going to church and being involved in activities and programs. This is not always so. I support being part of a fellowship and going to church, but church must also be at home. If your children are living with you, let the children see God in you. Live holy like Anna the prophetess or like the wife who lost her prophet husband. It may not be easy to live holy, but it is more beneficial.

Putting God first is allowing Him to be the CEO of the homes, our lives, and the lives of our children. Unfortunately, most single mothers put their children and careers in rivalry with God. They take life that should be given to God and put it in their activities. When the children and desires of single mothers are put before

God, then He has no choice but watch and wait. Putting God in a box like this opens the door for the enemy to come in. In other words, single mothers are responsible for transferring either a curse or a blessing to their children based on the position of God in their lives. When single mothers allow God to have no rival in their homes and lives, God will be their Provider and a Father to their children.

Setting a time for family devotion is necessary and beneficial. Start gradually and improve. I have seen beautiful testimonies of what God has done in the lives of vulnerable, God-fearing single mothers. Great leaders have emerged out of the homes of single motherhood, because God was the source of help throughout the challenges that come with such a situation.

FAMILY

God is very concerned about the family. God called Abraham, because He knew that Abraham was going to teach his children His ways. God wants every home to be a picture of Heaven, as it is stated in the Lord's prayer: "Thy kingdom come, Thy will be done in earth, as it is in heaven" (Matthew 6:10). In other words, a parent needs to be the reflection of the image of God in the house.

Make time for your children. Beware of people who want to get you involved in everything under the sun and leave you with no time for your kids. Remember that you are single, and time management must be important to you. Learn to say no and mean it.

Single parents, you need to spend time ministering to your children naturally as well as spiritually. You need to do things outside of the church building with your children. Be creative in developing less expensive, fun, and developmental activities for your kids. Purpose to do preliminary planning if the occasion requires more financial support.

Develop a loving relationship with your children. If you have never seen or caught your teenagers unexpectedly reading the Scriptures or praying on their own, you know it is time for you to minister to them. If children are curious about other things, they can be curious about the matters of God. Design your family time and activities according to a God-fearing way that works for you. Never ignore your kids for your own pleasure. Minimize going to places where kids are not allowed for fun activities. If you bond with your kids, they will be thankful, and you will enjoy them.

FORSAKE

Sometimes, the prerequisite to moving forward is to forsake certain habits. You need to forsake things that are robbing you of life, as well as any lifestyles that are contrary to the will and Word of God.

Avoid reading things into Scriptures that are opposed to the character of God. For example, believing God for a mate and living in sexual sin can affect a potential future relationship. Change is necessary in this area for those involved in fornication. You cannot live in sin and expect God to bring you the best. Stop living in tolerance outside the will of God.

Unfortunately, most Christians live in tolerance. They live and tolerate anything as long as it does not appear to have immediate judgment on their lives, not minding the long-term, destructive consequences. The Bible instructs us to come out of the world and sinful lifestyles. It did not instruct us to bring the world to the church. Although Jesus meets us where we are, after a new beginning in Christ, old things must pass away. Pray to God to help you come out of things that are against His Word.

FORWARD

Single mothers need to understand that it is God's will for them to go forward in life. In order for this to happen, they should begin to look forward to the promise of abundant life. Looking forward is looking at what God wants you to do, it is looking at your potential, and it is looking at your creativity and talents. This will cause you to experience the full life of Christ. It is sad to know that many single mothers are still looking backwards. They are looking at their pain and failures. I encourage you to look forward and receive the favor of

God. The devil is concerned about keeping you in your past, but God is concerned about your future. If there is any sin involved, repent of it and move forward.

FORGIVE

A lot of single mothers will never enter into God's rest because of unforgiveness. Unforgiveness is killing people on a daily basis. It will destroy your relationship with God and stop the blessing for your children.

Unforgiveness binds people in the spirit realm. God will not withold your blessing when you are binding someone else. Let go of certain people. I encourage you to lose your baby's father who abused and took advantage of you, along with any others in your life who have done so.

Remember that forgiveness is the first principle of Christianity (Ephesians 4:32). Receive grace through forgiveness. It is not easy, but it is beneficial to you. Forgiveness brings your life back to you. It takes your life from pain and anger and gives it back to you. Take your life from that hurt and frustration, and let God use your life.

FORGET

It is not always easy to forget the past when it has been so painful and destructive. For the Apostle Paul said, "but this one thing I do, forgetting those things which are behind, and reaching forth unto those things which are before" (Philippians 3:13b). Fight to move away from things that will remind you about your negative past. The devil specializes in reminding us about our bygone days. Martin Luther said, "You cannot keep birds from flying over your head but you can keep them from building a nest in your hair." This means that you have the ability to deal with negative thoughts that come to your mind.

The Bible gave us specific instructions to deal with any negativity:

> **Casting down imaginations, and every high thing that exalteth itself against the knowledge of God, and bringing into captivity every thought to the obedience of Christ**
>
> **2 Corinthians 10:5**

You have got to open your mouth and speak the Word of God against that negative past. Cast it down with the Word of God. Speak to yourself what God says about you.

Focus

Focus is knowing what you want out of this life and following that want. People who don't know what they want lack the ability to focus. Such people jump on every train that comes their way and open their ears to all trash. We should understand that God does not operate in confusion.

I encourage all single mothers to use this powerful weapon of focus. This will help them to focus on the solution and not the problem; to focus on what's in front of them and not on what's behind them. When you focus, you will be able to discipline your life. It is very difficult to achieve any goal without discipline.

Again, remember that focus is a powerful weapon. It helps change lives.

Freedom

You need to understand that you are free indeed, because Christ has set you free (John 8:36). You are free from your failures and your past. When you are in Jesus Christ, you are not condemned. You are free to succeed and move forward. Do not let situations or problems blind you. Understand your freedom. You are free to do the will of God. Freedom in Christ means that your life is not enslaved by systems, people, things, pleasures, and sins.

FIND

Don't sit down and wait for your problems to solve themselves. Always remember that with God, all things are possible (Matthew 19:26). This means that there is always a possibility.

Single mothers, find ways to accomplish your dreams, find ways to get help for your children, and find ways to reach your goals. There is always a way. Support groups are available to you. Make use of them. Ask God to open the door, and He will do just that.

FAITH

Faith is something no one can take from you. It is the greatest and indestructible weapon that one can have. "Faith is the substance of things hoped for, the evidence of things not seen" (Hebrews 11:1). When you have faith, you have the substance of what you need. Though there may not be evidence for what you are hoping for, the substance is the evidence in your hope.

You should fight the good fight of faith (1 Timothy 6:12). Fight to live the Christian faith. This is of great significance, because our lifestyles affect the level of our faith, and without faith, it is impossible to please God (Hebrews 11:6).

The results of our faith depend on our actions of trust in God. Without love for God and people, your faith will not work.

FASTING

Fasting is more effective in the life of a praying Christian. I did not state prayer in its own category, because prayer is supposed to be part of the life of any Christian. If you are a Christian, you should always pray.

Some hindrances are spiritual, and therefore, we need a spiritual force to remove such obstacles. Fasting involves denying ourselves of regular pleasures so that the Spirit of God will have control over our lives. When this happens, we are no longer controlled by the human spirit, but, instead, we are guided by the spirit of God. The Spirit of God comes with the power of God. It is this power that breaks the yoke and gives us authority over a situation.

Fasting takes our lives out of the natural and places them in the supernatural. It takes life from flesh to spirit. It helps us grow spiritually.

FELLOWSHIP

God created us, first of all, to have fellowship with Him and then with one another. Because of past experiences, many people have closed their borders and are living within themselves. Such lifestyles will limit one's potential and ability to attain success.

Single mother, you may be a super woman and may think you don't need any help from anyone, but God never created us to be independent. God wants us to know how to fellowship with Him first, then we can know how to fellowship with others. Sometimes, you may come across like a mean and crazy person to those who lack compassion, but this should not stop you from reaching out.

God has put everything we need here on earth. Since it is impossible for one person to have everything, therefore, we need one another. Fellowship allows us to share the favor of God in the lives of others. What we need is already here. God will connect us through fellowship to people who have what we need. Single mothers who are praying to God for a husband need to ask Him to help them know how to relate to the potential husband whom God sends their way.

Don't be so angry with men just because some men have hurt you in the past. God did not tell those people to hurt you; they hurt you because of sin in their lives. Allow God to let you smile and be friendly again. This does not mean that the past should repeat itself.

It is of great importance for a Christian to be in fellowship with other Christians. This will help a Christian to be stronger in the Lord. A true Christian fellowship should protect, support, build up, encourage, and strengthen everyone involved. This kind of fellowship should be like the best family you have ever had.

FURNISH

It is of great importance to be generous. Learn to be generous in the work of God. Trying to stay away from supporting the work of God financially doesn't help. Pay your tithes, and God will open the windows of Heaven and pour you out a blessing.

Be kind to the people you come across on a daily basis. Find little ways to help others. Always understand that being kind is sowing a good seed. Do not remain in bitterness and resentment and expect people to be kind to you. You should be nice and kind; whether people return it or not, it doesn't matter. God will bless you. You will be surprised how God will bless you from being kind to people without expecting anything in return.

FIGHT

"Fight the good fight of faith, lay hold on eternal life, whereunto thou art also called, and hast professed a good profession before many witnesses" (1 Timothy 6:12). The only battle we have to fight in this life is the fight of faith. Jesus has overcome and won the victory for us in all areas of our lives (John 16:33). We have to fight through faith and believe what Jesus has accomplished for us.

Every Christian is in a daily battle of faith. Faith is needed to move on and forward, and it is required to stay focused. Every Christian needs faith to stop the demons of their past from interrupting their new life in Christ. Faith is necessary to depend on God to provide for us and our children, and it is needed so that we believe that it shall be well with us. Prayer increases faith that leads to dependence on God. Praying, reading the Word regularly, and living in the presence of God are all part of the daily life of faith. Continue the fight of faith until death.

FINALLY

> **Finally, my brethren [single mothers], be strong in the Lord, and in the power of his might**
>
> **Ephesians 6:10**

When it comes to being strong, the Bible gives you no option. The word "be" expresses who someone really is. In other words, you have no choice but to be strong. You are not what you think you are; you are strong. That's what you are. When you are broke, be strong. When you are sick, be strong. When you are going through difficulties, be strong.

Be strong! Be strong! Be strong!

John K Genda

You have so much strength in Christ that you are not even aware of. You are strong in Christ.

ABOUT THE AUTHOR

It is not about the author, but about the cross of Jesus Christ. Therefore, these pages are only for informational purposes for the curious.

The author desires readers to view him as one who was once bound and controlled by the prince and power of the air and walked according to the course of this world, the spirit that now worketh in the children of disobedience (Ephesians 2:2). He was unfit and unworthy to take the cross and undeserving of grace, but the grace of God, which carries salvation to all, still appeared to him through a God Who so dearly loves him and gave His only Son for him (John 3:16). His unworthiness of the grace, which has been so freely poured on him, makes him see himself as the least among the saints to whom this grace was given to preach the unsearchable riches of Christ (Ephesians 3:8). His greatest accomplishment is the acceptance of this unmerited grace through repentance.

The author lives in western Maryland with his family and is a citizen of God's kingdom. His current spiritual address within the body of

Christ is Virginia Avenue Church of God, where he leads the prayer ministry.

John Genda's main focus areas of ministries are:

- *HOPAC (Household of Parents and Children)* - Helps parents and children understand their God-given responsibilities to each other and how to perform them in a balanced and healthy manner.
- *POG (Presence of God)* - The desperation of the early church to pursue the life of God as recorded in Acts chapter two, resulting in true fellowship with one another and with God, transmitted life to a dead world.
- *BEAM (Backyard Evangelism and Missions)* - BEAM helps churches to reach out to as many people as possible within the one-mile radius of their location intentionally and regularly.
- *FOHBAC (Fellowship of Holy Born Again Christians)* – Encouraging the fellowship of born-again Christians who believe in preaching against sin and promoting holy living.

Although the author is ordained and holds degrees in Biblical Studies, Paralegal Studies, Cybersecurity, and multiple certifications, he has no glory in such accomplishments. He counts all things as dung for the sake of the humble cross of Christ, not to be boastful of any status (Philippians 3:8).

The author prays not to be in the sad, empty state of placing much emphasis on things of vanity as human status and accomplishments, as stated by the preacher: "Vanity of vanities, saith the Preacher, vanity of vanities; all is vanity" (Ecclesiastes 1:2). He is humbled to continually pursue the cross.

He is the organizer of CLEAN PAGE fellowship, an association of individuals who believe in pursuing what God wants and encouraging others to do likewise. Also, he offers free cross life leadership training for startup churches and young people free of charge.

Please visit *www.johngenda.org* for further information.

www.ingramcontent.com/pod-product-compliance
Lightning Source LLC
Chambersburg PA
CBHW061342040426
42444CB00011B/3043